"Retrace your steps" in Ocean City!

[signature]

OCEAN CITY
MARYLAND

Captured Memories

Photography By Roger Miller
Writing By Chris Bohaska

IMAGE PUBLISHING, LTD.

IMAGE PUBLISHING, LTD.
1411 Hollins Street/Union Square
301-566-1222　　Baltimore, Maryland 21223　　FAX 301-233-1241

CREDITS

PHOTOGRAPHY: ROGER MILLER
TEXT: CHRIS BOHASKA
DESIGN: DAVID MILLER
PHOTOGRAPHY EDITING: ROGER MILLER
TEXT EDITING: CHRIS BOHASKA
　　　　　　　　MARTHA CLEMENTS
TYPESETTING & LAYOUTS: DELTA GRAPHICS, INC.,
　　　　　　　　TIMONIUM, MD.
COLOR SEPARATIONS: COLOURSPLENDOR GRAPHICS,
　　　　　　　　HONG KONG
PRINTING: HONG KONG
　　　　　　　　BY SHINY OFFSET PRINTING CO., LTD.

COPYRIGHT INFORMATION

© 1989 by Image Publishing, Ltd. Compilation and writing. All rights reserved.

© 1989 by Roger Miller, Photographer. All rights reserved.

All rights reserved. No part of this book may be reproduced or transmitted in any form or by any means, electronic or mechanical, including photocopying or recording, or by any information storage and retrieval system, without permission in writing from the publisher.

PUBLISHING INFORMATION

First printing 1989
Library of Congress Catalog Card Number: 89-083378
ISBN# 0-91189716-X

ORDERS

For direct orders please call or write for specific cost, postage and handling to the above address. Discount available for stores and institutions, minimum orders required.

DEDICATION

NANCY

To a close friend and business associate for years. Someone who has believed in my photography and books even when the "numbers" didn't justify that belief.

Your advice, efforts and support in getting my "numbers" where they should be is finally reaping success. Without your efforts my books wouldn't continue to exist. So this book is for you! Much thanks.
Roger Miller 8-9-89

SPECIAL THANKS

I would like to thank everyone who had a part in this project. I would especially like to thank the following:

A special thanks to all the people and businesses in Ocean City. Without their hard work and dedication in making Ocean City a world class resort this book would not be possible.

To **Roland E. Powell**, Mayor of Ocean City, I would like to thank him for his support and for writing the foreword to the book.

A special thanks to **Robert A. Rothermel Jr.**, Executive Director of Tourism and the Ocean City Convention Center, for his advice and assistance. Without his foresight and effort this book would not exist.

To **Martha O. Clements**, Director of Public Relations, for the town of **Ocean City**. A very special thanks for her day to day advice and support on this book. Not only did you get me straight on all the details, but you kept all of us laughing hysterically.

Finally a very special thanks to the following for their hospitality, advice and support on the Ocean City book: Annabell Plummer of Annabell's; Sally Rutka of the Lankford Hotel; Kate Bunting of the Belmont-Hearne Hotel; Andrea Ullrich and Thelma Conner of Dunes Manor Hotel; Betsy Cohill of the Harrison Group; Sam Cook and Fred Wise of The Carousel Hotel; Dr. Berger and Stan Kahn of the Sheraton; Captain Joe Velenza of the "Therapy;" Mr. John Fager of the Coconut Malorie; Shirley Phillips of Phillips Restaurants; Jan Smith of the Ramada Inn; Hal Glick of Moore, Warfield and Glick, as well as everyone else who was so kind in helping me do this book.
Roger Miller 8-9-89

The sun rises from the east, streaking the waves that roll to the shore a brilliant shade of orange. Moments like these, with the sand and rolling surf, are the magnet that draw people to Ocean City again and again.

With the sand soft and cool beneath their feet, a couple and their baby slip silently along the wide, wind-blown, sandy beach in Old Town. Early morning hours are a perfect time for a peaceful stroll and quiet contemplation.

TABLE OF CONTENTS

Mayor's Foreword	6
Introduction	8
History	10
Old Town	12
Midtown	28
North Ocean City	36
Bayside	42
Recreation	46
Accommodations	54
Surrounding Areas	68

FOREWORD

Ocean City and its ten miles of clean, white beach belongs to everyone. Any visitor who crosses one of the bridges onto this special island has a claim to its beauty, excitement and charm.

Since its founding in 1875, the small fishing village has made a gradual transformation into one of the most popular vacation spots for many Marylanders as well as visitors from other states on the east coast. Some of these visitors are part of a tradition that has been passed on for generations. These people have spent their summer vacations growing up in Ocean City and have many fond memories of their times at the beach. Now they are bringing their children to the beach and the tradition continues.

As more and more people discover Ocean City, we are pleased that we can provide so many activities and forms of entertainment. Naturally, fishing and water sports are our most popular activities, with Ocean City proudly claiming the title as the "White Marlin Capital of the World." Recreational boating, water skiing, jet skiing, parasailing and windsurfing are just a few of the many sports available on the ocean and bay. Maryland's largest amusement parks are in Ocean City, too, and vacationers of all ages enjoy the rides, the miniature golf courses and the atmosphere at these popular sites.

Of course, no trip to Ocean City would be complete without a visit to our renowned Boardwalk. You can visit the many shops and eateries along the "boards," or take a seat on the Boardwalk train and get a spectacular view of the beach and ocean while relaxing and window shopping.

As a natural progression to the demands of a greater number of visitors, Ocean City has grown by leaps and bounds. Hotels, motels, condominiums, restaurants and shopping malls have all sprung up along Coastal Highway. Improvements and beautification to the highway have greatly improved the appearance and traffic flow on Ocean City's main thoroughfare. Nestled among the condominiums and hotels, though, you can still find quaint cottages and historic rooming houses. Ownership in condominiums has also increased visits to Ocean City all year 'round.

No longer a secret, many people are discovering that Ocean City has just as much to offer in the fall, spring and winter as it does in the summer. The traditional Sunfest held in September each year kicks off Ocean City's second season and has become quite an attraction. No matter what season you choose to visit Ocean City, you won't be disappointed.

It's been a pleasure to take part in a production such as this pictoral of Ocean City captured by Roger Miller in this wonderful volume of photographs. As you leaf through the pages, the pictures may stimulate a fond memory of a day spent at the beach with the kids, or an evening on the Boardwalk with someone special. Whatever the thought or memory, you can be assured that Ocean City will be here for generations to come. Just as Ocean City holds a special place in the hearts of those of us who call it home, we are pleased that so many find their second home on this beautiful island. We are proud to share it!

Roland E. Powell
Mayor

Fishing. The original attraction to this beautiful barrier island. Above, a charter boat crosses the calm, evening waters of the inlet that connects Sinepuxent Bay with the Atlantic Ocean. Formed by a vicious Northeaster in 1933, the inlet provides passage from the safe harbors of Ocean City's many bays to the Atlantic.

INTRODUCTION

I can still remember one of my first trips to Ocean City when I was a child. I guess I was about ten or eleven years old, sitting restlessly in the back-seat of my parent's gigantic green station wagon. I was probably arguing with my sister, looking for something to occupy my time. The thrill of crossing the Bay Bridge had long since worn off and my anticipation of reaching the beach had been dulled by the low, sandy flatlands of the Eastern Shore. Some twenty years later, I would discover the patches of dark, majestic evergreens, the quiet tidal creeks, the fertile farmlands and small, Southern-like towns would fascinate me; but back then, the stretch from the bay to the ocean was agonizing.

By the time we got to the Route 50 bridge to cross into Ocean City, the wide stretch of sand and the roaring call of the ocean beckoned me like a long, lost homeland. I was desperate to feel my feet squishing in the sand where it meets the ocean, the surf grabbing my ankles as it slides back out into the vast expanse of water. But my father, as if to test my patience even more, slowed the car down to a crawl as he and my mother traded stories, reminiscing about their past visits. They remembered my grandfather perched along the guardrail of the bridge, the long brim of his favorite fishing cap mysteriously shadowing the content smile on his face, as he fished all day for "the big one." They were sure his ghost was there, waiting among the row of fishermen we now saw lining the bridge. That had always been his vision of heaven – standing there with his rod resting on the rail, waiting patiently for a moment of life to invigorate his line.

Now when you enter the city, whether by Route 50 or the newer Route 90, you discover the horizon has changed. After dusk, Ocean City greets you with a glittering string of lights, doubly magnificent as they reflect in the waters of the bay. To the north, the skyline rises from the horizon and one can't help but be captivated by the spirit of what Ocean City has become. Like the waves, the night here moves to a pace and rhythm of its own. The lights tell you that Ocean City is alive with excitement and endless possibilities.

But, no matter how many times I cross these bridges and see the light show, I still slow down just a little and look at the row of fishermen lining the edges. I wonder how many ghosts tramp this shore, treading softly through their sandy heaven. And now, after almost two dozen summers in Ocean City, I find that I have ghosts and stories of my own, just like my parents do. In the car next to me – smaller, but a station wagon nonetheless – my eyes fall on a family a lot like mine. Parents navigate in front, arms extended in vain as they try to point out everything at once. In the back seat, crowded by the usual beach supplies – extra towels, a bright orange and yellow kite, even a couple of inflated beach balls (as if there won't be time to blow them up when they hit the beach) – sit two children entranced, eyes wide, with the magical land of lights, sand and sea. Looking at them, I can still recall that same feeling I had gazing at this somewhat different scene, two decades ago.

It doesn't take much to note the changes that have taken place here in the last twenty years; just a glance at the high-rise condos emphasizes that. But walk down into Old Town Ocean City and I dare you to not be that kid again, racing through t-shirt shops, a cup of vinegar-soaked fries in your hand. Or survey the amusement park as it lights up the sky like a gigantic, false aurora. No matter how many times you've been here, the sheer size of the ocean still surprises and the beach seems to stretch on forever, luring the lovers of the salt air onto its sunwarmed sand. The procession of sunning and swimming begins all over again and the crowd on the boardwalk swells with each passing hour. Seagulls cry overhead as you rush into the breaking surf, find your depth and then ride a wave back into shore.

The mix of change and permanence here is unique, and the town somehow carries it well. There is a wonderfully strange sense of deja vu, as you hurry down the boardwalk with the salty ocean breeze brushing in your hair. Memories come easy, crowding the mind like the lights and the curious crowd the boardwalk, looking for something new in a nook or hidden street. This is what a vacation town is supposed to be: a place where there's always something new to discover while you retrace the steps of your past.

A lone seagull rests atop a piling as it surveys the sunrise on the horizon. Quieted in the morning by the restful lull of the rolling ocean water, seagulls provide a neverending burst of joyous noise as they flirt and play with friendly visitors during the day.

HISTORY

Ocean City is a barrier island that stretches ten miles from the Sinepuxent Bay at the south end, to the Delaware line at the north. The barren, windswept land was used for years primarily as grazing land, but more significantly, as an area for a handful of fishermen who ventured by rowboat from the mainland to the island to partake in their version of "the better life."

Witnessing the island's popularity with visiting fishermen and others, Isaac C. Coffin, a local farmer, built the first structure on the island in 1869, "The Rhode Island Inn." A few years later, in the early 1870's, a group of developers formed the Sinepuxent Bay Corporation and secured land through grants and gifts. The families of the group regularly traveled by stagecoach and carriage to the mostly vacant island, crossing the waterway to it in small boats. They had at least two early names for the island, referring to it as "The Ladies Resort to the Ocean" (in an attempt to attract more women to the island) and "The Rhode Island Inn Resort."

More hotels began to spring up in the early 1870's: the Atlantic, the Seaside and Congress Hall, while cottages were also being built, both as private residences and to accommodate visitors. When a single investor deeded fifty acres of land in 1875, a surveyor mapped out the town, establishing the north and south boundary lines (now known as N. and S. Division Streets) and the town officially became Ocean City.

Another major step in Ocean City's development took place in 1879 when the railroad crossed the Sinepuxent Bay to the depot on Baltimore Avenue. By 1900, Ocean City could boast two general stores, a post office, two churches and an amusement center. A visitor during the first two decades of the century was bound to see a portrait of the resort town that was straight out of an impressionist painting: ladies carrying parasols and men wearing straw hats spending sunny afternoons strolling the boardwalk or pedalling three-wheeled carts. Ocean bathing was permitted at the Life Saving Station at Caroline Street. It was a boom time for the resort town.

Boardwalk construction took place during this time. The two-block boardwalk was firmly anchored for the warm weather, then the boards would be removed and stored away each winter until the next spring when it was put back in place again. The first permanent boardwalk was installed in 1912.

The first bridge for motor travelers was opened in 1918. During the first two decades of the century, the town had spread steadily north to about Sixth Street (there were a few scattered buildings further north); but growth was restricted, first during World War I and then even more so during the depression.

In August 1933, a savage hurricane ripped through Ocean City, leveling many oceanfront buildings and destroying large sections of the boardwalk. The tides from the Northeaster were so strong that the ocean cut an inlet to the Sinepuxent Bay that now separates Ocean City from Assateague Island and also serves as the southern terminus of the boardwalk. It wasn't all bad news though, as the inlet was navigable when the storm subsided and it opened a channel to the ocean for both commercial and sportfishing. Using the bay as a safe harbor, fishermen could quickly make their way to the Atlantic. Thanks to the inlet's improving conditions for deep sea fishing, Ocean City soon became known as "The White Marlin Capital of the World."

After the storm, a rock jetty was built at the inlet by the Army Corps of Engineers to protect the oceanfront buildings. One of the by-products was that large deposits of sand, resulting from the jetty, widened the beach by nearly ten times to its current width.

More growth took place after World War II, and with the completion of the first span of the Chesapeake Bay Bridge in 1952, Ocean City became hours closer to the metropolitan areas of Baltimore and Washington, D.C. Since then, development has become increasingly rapid. With this development has come increased popularity in the resort's appeal and not even a devastating storm in March 1962 could dampen the spirits of the inhabitants. By the opening of the summer season that year, much of the boardwalk and most of the $20 million in damages had been rebuilt or restored.

Since that remarkable recovery, the vitality and determination of Ocean City has been seen time after time with projects like the Beach Replenishment Program, in which Ocean City strives to continue its reputation as a popular vacation resort on the east coast.

A rock jetty built at the inlet after the storm of 1933 resulted in massive sand deposits that widened Old Town's beaches nearly ten times to their present width. From a distance, the beach seems to stretch north as far as the ocean stretches east. This, above all, is Ocean City's most spectacular natural attraction.

OLD TOWN

This is where it all began over one hundred years ago. Old Town. Where the beach is the widest, where the old hotels still look past the boardwalk, past the sand and into the blue-grey horizon of the Atlantic. The Plim Plaza, the Shoreham, the Atlantic, the Lankford, the Commander and Harrison Hall – these are a few of the grand old hotels whose names have woven themselves into the minds and histories of the visitors here at Ocean City. Comfortable, relaxed places like the Belmont-Hearne and the George Washington; quaint Bed and Breakfasts like Annabell's and His Honor's Place. Hotels and cottages that seem like they have always been here with the sand, the salty air, and the sunrise.

Even right on the boardwalk, the atmosphere in Old Town is relaxed and festive. Guests sit back on the veranda and rock slowly with the rhythm of the ocean. The cool, summer breeze sweeps off the water as they engage in soft talk and one of the town's oldest and most popular activities: people watching. A never-ending caravan of people stroll up and down the boardwalk all day. There's a collective buzz to the crowd, and if you look closely, you can see that each person reacts differently to the sensory bombardment of the surroundings. You can see children, their eyes alive, trying to take it all in. Most adults are more calm, relaxed, many with a small smile of contentment on their faces for having finally made it through another year of work. The boardwalk train passes, bells ring, and a whole new buzz consumes the old one. It's a constant world of movement and sound.

With darkness, a new city comes to life, as the lights of the shops and amusement parks push back the night and a second day begins on the boards. Crowds jam the boardwalk, sampling the traditional beach fare: french fries from Thrasher's, taffy from Dolle's or caramel popcorn from Fisher's. Anything you can eat while walking is preferred. For some reason, the pace, the sights and the sounds make it all taste better.

Down the boardwalk, the lights of amusement parks spin and whirl through the sky. It's much the same now as it was several decades ago – the rides are faster, there are more lights – but the spirit remains the same. There's a double Ferris wheel on the pier and all sorts of other technologically-marvelous, stomach-churning loops and rides, but the traditional still survives and flourishes. Trimper's Rides, on the boardwalk, a family business for generations, still features one of the country's oldest operating wooden carousels and a spectacular fun house.

And on the pier, you can still hear the fast-paced rhythms of the carnival as the barkers seduce the passersby into the games that look so easy – pitching softballs at bottles, tossing darts at balloons and rings at various prizes – but turn out to be a frustrating challenge. All for a stuffed animal and a little showing off.

For something completely modern, step into Photon, where you can search for both your friends and enemies, in a futuristic world of glowing red and blue lights. It's a game of survival – a life-size, three-dimensional video game that you can actually walk through.

Of course if you need to relax from the pace of all these attractions, take a stroll on the boardwalk. At the southern end stands a stunning white Victorian structure that has stood in Ocean City since 1891. It's the Ocean City Life Saving Station, now a museum that proudly displays the history of the resort town. Take a look inside where you'll find memorabilia of the sea and Ocean City. There are lifesaving boats and old-time bathing suits, as well as five saltwater aquariums. A wall of sea-going maps point to boats that are sunk off the coast.

North, up the boardwalk, you may see huge sand castles or a nightly biblical sand sculpture. One sand castle recently built was over three stories high, with plans for an even larger one to be built in the future.

Old Town is the heart of Ocean City – the place where it all began. There are changes here, to be sure, but the wide beach and crashing waves are the same, as is the carnival atmosphere on the boards at night. Walk down these boards and you'll feel young – staring in awe at the light show before you, feeling the rush of the crowd and warmth of the night.

On holidays – like Memorial Day, the Fourth of July and Labor Day – the sun-warmed, sandy beach and the cool playful surf attract thousands of worshippers of the sun, sand and sea. On other days, particularly weekdays, the crowds thin out and the beach seems more private and less hectic. White cotton-like clouds watch over the ocean and offer up cool, salty breezes that are good for the body and the mind.

Each day on the beach begins with the careful symmetry of colorful umbrellas (above). As the day progresses, though, scores of umbrellas are opened, forming a helter-skelter, polka-dot pattern on the sun-drenched beach (below).

Typical of the hotels, homes and cottages in Old Town, the long porches and wide verandas provide an age old tradition in Ocean City. Sitting under the cool shade of the brightly striped awnings, visitors can sit back and relax in tall-backed rockers while the world seems to pass by before them.

Ocean City's oldest and most venerable hotels line the boardwalk in Old Town, gazing out on the beach and the ocean. Their histories are interwoven with the history of the resort town itself. The Lankford (below), rises from the beach like a majestic Southern plantation.

Ocean City's City Hall (above), a restored schoolhouse built in 1915, now acts as the center of Ocean City's government. After a series of land grants were obtained and roads were laid out, the island was officially named Ocean City in 1875. Before the development of Upper Ocean City, the town was practically a ghost town from Labor Day to Memorial Day. A few years ago, scenes like this one (below) – Ocean City covered in a blanket of snow – would have been unknown to most vacationers.

The Ocean City Life Saving Station stands vigil over the boardwalk at the inlet. Built in 1891, it is now a museum dedicated to the history of the town and to ocean life. The stunning Victorian clapboard structure is home to life saving boats and old beach fashions as well as several saltwater fish tanks. Look among the exhibits for maps of boats sunk off the coast, or gaze at the remarkable miniatures of Ocean City buildings that are part of this museum's collection.

The boardwalk runs from the inlet, at the south end, all the way up to 27th Street, at the north. Every inch of it is packed with exciting shops, like the Kite Loft (below), eateries, hotels and motels. Using the boardwalk train, which rides the entire distance (above), is an easy way to discover all the charms of the boards.

It seems that crowds pack the boardwalk no matter what time of day you visit. At night, make your way down to the amusement parks at the south end, or maybe ride a bicycle in the morning through Midtown.

Sand sculpture has become a gigantic attraction at the beach in recent years. The thirty foot tall sandcastle (above), took five professionals and thirty volunteers eleven days to construct. After completion, they held workshops for the public on the art of sandcastle building. Biblical sand sculpture (below), is changed nightly in front of the Plim Plaza on 2nd Street.

When you're on the boardwalk, sample the traditional cuisine of Ocean City's famous fast foods. Whether it's a slice of pizza from The Dough Roller, saltwater taffy from Dolle's or Candy Kitchen, or fries from Thrasher's, you're bound to find something scrumptious here.

Two of the more traditional scenes at Ocean City's Amusement Parks. Above, rows of stuffed animals hang from every wall and ceiling, waiting to be claimed by skillful (and lucky) pitchers of rings, balls and darts. Below is an endless array of pinball and other electronic games, ringing and buzzing in a frenzy of noise.

Some of the newer additions on the boardwalk, near the pier, are Photon and Riptide On The Pier. The giant waterslide is a swirling, round-a-bout cascade of water, falling dozens of feet into a pool of water. Photon (below), is a space age video game, where with a passport and a ticket, you and your friends can step into an imaginary planet with a sophisticated system of lights, mazes and electronic gear.

Trimper's Rides, an amusement park on the south end of the boardwalk, has been an Ocean City favorite for generations. The park features a series of looping, stomach-churning rides, a spectacular fun house and one of the country's oldest operating wooden carousels (above).

The Pier Amusements, located on the pier near the inlet at the southern end of the boardwalk, boasts a plethora of lightening fast rides as well as a spectacular light show that turns the night-time sky into an aurora of color. One of its most fascinating rides is a double carousel.

Looking past the dunes up along the stretch of beach in Midtown, one can see the more modern facades of hotels and condos that line the beach. Coastal Highway widens in this area but the beach, which is less crowded here, is still the number one attraction.

MIDTOWN

Walking north along the boardwalk, one notices a slow and subtle change in the landscape that begins around Fifteenth Street. The hotels and motels through this stretch are newer and some are larger than their counterparts in Old Town. Walking along the beach, one sees the rows of rooms and balconies facing east like miniature temples to the ocean and gorgeous sunrises. Places like Castle in the Sand, Dunes Manor and the Quality Inn stand taller and are more spaciously separated from their surroundings than hotels in the older parts of town.

On the boards, as well as the beach, the crowds thin out somewhat. It's easier to stake a claim to a larger piece of the beach here and bicycle riding on the boardwalk is less stressful, thanks to fewer hazards. What's lost in pace and excitement here is gained in a sense of space and a stronger family atmosphere.

Although the beach is still the main event in Midtown, the focus on entertainment shifts to the Coastal Highway, which widens here to eight lanes. Phillip's Crab House, one of the country's largest restaurants, has been a staple in Midtown for years.

At 40th Street, the Convention Center majestically overlooks Coastal Highway to the east and the Isle of Wight Bay to the west. The spacious center architecturally reflects the more modern face of condos and motels in this area, and it is host to conventions, arts and crafts shows and big band dances. It also brings nationally-known acts like Kenny Rogers, the Smothers Brothers and Bill Cosby to town. Any tidbit of information on Ocean City is available here at the Visitor Information Center, and the hospitality and warmth of the people reflects the small town Eastern Shore feeling that never seems to get lost in Ocean City, even during the most frantic times.

Scattered along Coastal Highway, one can find all kinds of family entertainment, from watersports to miniature golf. And, after a day on the beach, nothing beats a hearty dinner or buffet at one of the many fine restaurants. Of course, if you get too relaxed, you can plunder the Jolly Roger Amusement Park, where children of all ages can scamper about under the lights, sampling the go-carts, an assortment of roller coasters and other screamfest rides. Look for the Italian double carousel, one of the park's more unique rides. For the squeamish, check out the dolphin show, highdive act or the petting zoo. Or you can wend your way through the uniquely decorated miniature golf courses that seem to wait for you on every other corner. Anywhere you go in Midtown, you're bound to find something to attract you.

On the bay side of Midtown, Fager's sumptious Lighthouse Club stands vigil over the bay and the Coconut Malorie Hotel adds a touch of luxury to Ocean City, luxury that is found in other major resorts all over the world.

Midtown is a transition area, a family style atmosphere between the non-stop action of Old Town and the private, elegant feel of Upper Ocean City. It's perfect for those who want a comfortable, more relaxed pace during their visit to the ocean.

In an endless cycle of the imagination, children build replicas of medieval castles along the edge of the surf. Once washed away, the building begins anew. Midtown offers a more calm, family atmosphere, where dreaming, young architects can practice for the future.

Looking along the beach in Midtown, one will see more open space than in Old Town. The northern end of the boardwalk ends here at 27th Street. The last half dozen blocks of the boards are perfect for bicycling or casual, slow-paced walking.

The Ocean City Convention Center stands majestically over Coastal Highway to the east and the Isle of Wight Bay to the west. Located in Midtown at 40th Street, the Center host conventions, dances, arts and crafts shows and other entertainment. Below, one visiting convention spreads out various displays in one of the building's spacious halls.

Besides being the host to large conventions (above), the Ocean City Convention Center is noted for bringing nationally-recognized acts like Robert Palmer, Kenny Rogers and Bill Cosby to town. Below, the Smothers Brothers play before a packed house.

The rooms in the Quality Inn Oceanfront, on 54th Street, look down upon a five-story atrium, filled with exotic plants and birds. Under the leaves of the palms and other plants, you can enjoy the pool, hot tubs or quiet walks over footbridges and garden paths.

The Dunes Manor Hotel captures the essence of early Ocean City seaside hotels with verandas and porches that face the beach. Located in Midtown, the Victorian-styled hotel offers oceanfront accommodations with old fashioned Eastern Shore hospitality. Tea is served daily by the hotel's owner, Mrs. Thelma Conner.

Looking east from across the bay, one can see the dramatic row of condominiums that have changed not only the landscape but the seasonal aspects of what was once only a "summer resort."

NORTH OCEAN CITY

It used to be that one would travel to the area north of 45th Street to "get away from it all." And, although North Ocean City still has a somewhat slower, more calm pace than Old Town, the area has changed rapidly in the last twenty years and has taken on a bold new life of its own.

Becoming part of the city proper in 1965, the first high rise condominium was completed in Ocean City in 1971. With the opening of Route 90 and the bridge that enters Ocean City at 60th Street, development of elegant hotels, breathtaking condos and first class restaurants has led to a transformation from the quiet, empty beaches to a stunning, bright-light display of a world-class resort town.

Thousands flock to the beach year-round where they can now enjoy Ocean City's famous seafood in elegantly styled restaurants. There's a private, quiet feel in North Ocean City, where families and older vacationers can stroll from the beach during the day to the boldly-lit streets for great food and entertainment at night. The Ramada Inn boasts a rooftop restaurant with one of the finest views in the city, as well as a lounge that seats over 400 and books nationally-known acts. Where the crazy hustle and bustle of the boardwalk in Old Town is infectious, the North Ocean City visitor will be pleasantly overwhelmed with the choice of shopping, eating and entertainment that takes place here not just on summer days and nights, but now all year long

Today, condominium owners travel to the beach in the spring, fall and winter, and the Gold Coast Mall as well as other shops, restaurants and malls all over Ocean City remain open during the "off season" rather than close at the first trace of cold. The fall closings once turned the resort into a virtual ghost town after Labor Day a few years ago, but no more.

The Sheraton Hotel, among others, offers plush hotel rooms, large convention facilities and first-class food service. The Carousel Hotel, also a convention property, has its mind on summer and winter, with the wide, sandy beaches outside and a year-round ice rink located inside.

Restaurants, like The Hobbit and The Landing, in North Ocean City, are casual yet elegant. Although they specialize in tasty seafood dishes, their menus contain choices that reflect the year-round atmosphere that now exists, thanks to North Ocean City.

Where Ocean City used to close shop just after Labor Day, the new development of the north end has changed shoulder seasons to a time when you can take advantage of great amenities. Just one glance at all the lights on during a fall evening proves that. And more people are discovering some of the dramatic fall and winter sunsets that descend on the bayside, now that they are not going home so soon.

Even with all the changes, the beach is still the common denominator. Nothing feels as refreshing as a spirited walk along the beach in November, when a crisp wind slaps color in your cheeks and, with pants rolled up to your knees, you dance on tip-toes between sand and surf, the startling cold splash of water on your feet. At night, the mood can be more serious, when you can dress up and enjoy the town: the lights, the food and the surroundings of North Ocean City.

Sponsored by the Sheraton, the Best Body On The Beach contest always draws a crowd. The popularity of the weekly contests have led to several different competitions throughout Ocean City.

Once virtually deserted, the beach in Upper Ocean City (above) is now alive with people who stay at the skyscraping condos and hotels at the north end of town. Footprints in the sand (below) betray the number of wanderers who awaken with the sun to venture out into the morning's brisk breeze and spectacular sunrise. Mornings on the beach are quiet and peaceful and a shared smile between like-minded hikers reminds us of the small-town ambience that Ocean City retains.

Housing options in Ocean City run the full spectrum from conservative to the ultra chic. Above is a year-round Bayside townhouse in Heron Harbor while below is an example of a two-story Ocean condo in Sea Watch. Moore, Warfield and Glick, Inc. – one of Ocean City's largest independently owned realtors – offers a wide selection of condos and townhouses throughout the Ocean City area.

Some of the most eye-catching designs of the condominiums are the geometric shapes of pyramids (above) and the rows of balconies (below), that provide a modern landscape in a city with old-fashioned qualities.

A big orange sun rests among the clouds on the bay after another long summer day. Dramatic sunsets are a common occurrence and can be witnessed from dozens of restaurants, bars and homes on the bayside of Ocean City.

BAYSIDE

Walk along the marsh grasses or sit with your feet dangling off a pier and you're bound to see fishermen, silhouetted in the early morning light, casting their lines into the bay. Water sports are the main attraction on the bayside of the island, whether it's the calm solitude of the lone fishermen or the rollicking bounce of a jet ski skimming through the shallow water, a white spray of water left in its wake.

Like Upper Ocean City, the bayside has developed rapidly in the last twenty years, but town houses are the norm over on this side. Prime waterfront lots allow inhabitants to enjoy the calm waters of the bay, and the brightly colored sails of the wind surfers, day-sailers and sleek catamarans can be seen filling the horizon. The various sails arc high off the water, instantly becoming a seascapist's dream. Parasailers hover overhead for those who want to get above it all, taking in Ocean City from 300-500 feet.

Of course, sportfishing, the initial reason for development in Ocean City, is still the main attraction here. Half a dozen "party boats" accommodate scores of fishermen and the curious into the bay, while deep sea charter boats make the trip out to the ocean early each morning in a quest for "the big ones." The charters go in search of Bluefish, Blue Marlin, Tuna, Dolphin and Shark. The most spectacular fish, though, is the White Marlin and the White Marlin Tournament, the most popular and most recognized fishing event in Ocean City, takes place each August.

Fishermen with more modest tastes line the Route 50 bridge for Flounder, Sea Bass and Sea Trout. It's a daily high tide vigil of the dedicated; the ritual of early risers and nature lovers. There's no doubt that fish are not the sole attraction to the sport. Ask any of the faithful and they'll tell you there is a special communion with the land and the sea that can only be experienced out in the waters and marshes of the bay.

Of course, no one can miss the crowds on piers and bulkheads pulling in lines loaded with Maryland's famous blue crabs. This local delicacy is abundant all over the bay side of Ocean City. Probably the only thing you can't catch out in the bay with a fishing line is the beer and Old Bay!

Off the beaten track, the developments on Bayside provide quiet harbor retreats for year-round enjoyment in Ocean City. Boats line the piers of townhouses along this stretch of waterfront property.

The low flat marshes on Bayside provide some of the most exciting opportunities for dramatic sunsets. Real estate on this side of the island is available for individual homes or townhomes, where owners can enjoy the amenities of an ocean vacation with the comfort of home.

A fishing boat cuts through the choppy seas of the Atlantic in winter. There are an endless variety of fish in the bay and the ocean that attract addicted anglers to Ocean City in all seasons. In fact, the success of the resort town is rooted in the popularity of sportfishing.

RECREATION

When you think about recreation in Ocean City, you've got to begin on the water. Ocean City is surrounded by all types of bodies of water, from the Atlantic Ocean to its string of bays, from its inlet to its creeks and marshes. Each body of water offers its own unique brand of entertainment and you can spend each day of your visit doing something different. Not only are there a wide variety of water activities available here, but the nature of the water provides specific areas for both the novice and the skilled.

Fishing is the obvious first choice in this area, and it is available in one form or another practically all year. Most sportfishing takes place between April and November, with each month offering a different type of fish to hook.

In early April, huge schools of Mackerel arrive from the south for fishermen who like to get an early start on the season. Bluefish, weighing up to twenty pounds, arrive next and inhabit the waters around Ocean City from late April until mid-December.

The most popular bay fish, the Flounder, arrives around the same time as the Bluefish. The "doormat-sized" Flounder are a special prize for angler's who dot the bays, as well as the bridges and piers in and around the town.

For those who can't resist the lure of the deep, big game fishing begins in late May with the arrival of the first big Shark. July through September is prime time, when charter boats head out to the Gulf Stream looking for Tuna, Wahoo, Dolphin, Blue Marlin and Ocean City's most prestigious fish – the White Marlin. The White Marlin Tournament takes place in August and is one of Ocean City's most venerable affairs.

If you prefer to keep your feet on solid ground, surf fishing season comes around just as the weather turns cooler and the crowds on the beach thin out. In the fall and winter, the beach becomes a fisherman's paradise when one can cast into the ocean for a wide variety of fish.

Crabbing is another gigantic favorite on bayside. There's nothing like coming home with a couple dozen of Maryland's famous blue crabs.

Boats for all types of fishing can be rented all over Ocean City while piers, bridges and bulkheads are too numerous to mention. Talk to someone at a local tackle shop; they're more than happy to sit back and tell you what's biting and where.

If you're not into fishing, you're sure to find something else to do on the water. The calm, shallow waters of the bay are perfect for water sports like windsurfing, jet skiing or sailing. Catamarans are great for leisure sailing enthusiasts. Sailors of the Assawoman and Isle of Wight Bays are bound to happen upon one of the quiet creeks or rivers connected to these bays where the fauna and wildlife in the marshes and on tiny islands never cease to be a special discovery.

The bays are also great for the novice windsurfer. A combination of surfing and sailing, this increasingly popular sport is a great way to enjoy the water. Advanced windsurfers can find the challenge of the Atlantic exhilarating, as they weave through the waves, sails pulsing in the wind like gigantic one-winged butterflies.

Ocean City is one of the only resorts on the East Coast to have a rotating beach system for surfers – one of the more traditional water sports on the Atlantic. Bodyboarding is another sport for the novice, when, like surfing, you feel like you're sailing over the waves.

Of course, if flying is what you desire, give parasailing a try. Seeing Ocean City from 300-500 feet is an experience that should not be missed, at least not for the strong-hearted.

One of the more unique and exciting activities in Ocean City is skindiving. The town recently sank a World War II submarine, the U.S.S. Blenny, twelve miles off the coast, where it has become a fishing reef and habitat for native underwater sea-life. There are a large number of other wrecks sunk off the coast of Ocean City for diving, too. The dive shops around town will be glad to give you plenty of information.

Golfing is the second most popular sport next to fishing, and Ocean City boasts four full-size golf courses with two more under construction. The town is also loaded with tennis courts, baseball and softball fields, lots for volleyball and skateboarding facilities.

Naturally, less strenuous, but recreation nonetheless, is lying on the beach, wading in the ocean and people watching. There are practically no skills necessary for any of these "sports" and the possibilities for challenge and excitement are endless.

One of the newer activities in water-sports is scuba diving. Ocean City recently sank a World War II submarine twelve miles off the coast. The sub, along with several other wrecks, provide a habitat for fish and other sea life. Above, a charter boat, oxygen tanks in tow, heads out into the Atlantic. There are also charters available for every form of fishing imaginable (below).

Surf fishing is a popular and relaxing way to spend a quiet evening on the bay (above). Surf fishing in the ocean is most popular beginning a few weeks after Labor Day. For the diehard sport fisherman, the White Marlin Tournament takes place in August. The noble fish, like the 222 pound Blue Marlin above, can be caught off the coast, and has made Ocean City famous for being "The White Marlin Capital of the World."

Windsurfing, or sail boarding, is an increasingly popular watersport. The shallow Isle of Wight and Assawoman Bays are just right for the beginner (below). The ocean is more suited for the experienced windsurfer, as well as the surfer, who delicately maneuvers the rolling water into the shore (above).

The bays, on the west side of Ocean City, are ideal for a variety of water sports. The calm and shallow waters provide optimum conditions for catamaran races (below) or jet skiing. A jet ski (above) skims across the surface of the bay, leaving a spray of water in its wake.

Golfing is considered Ocean City's second most popular sport, behind fishing. Ocean Pines Golf Course, one of several courses in and around town, was designed by Robert Trent Jones, one of the world's foremost golf course architects. Opened in 1971, the PGA championship course is noted for incorporating the lush surroundings of Ocean Pines into its design.

Take a half-day or an evening cruise on Therapy. The 34 foot Crealock Cutter takes a maximum of six passengers into the calm Atlantic from Ocean City to Assateague. You'll see the famous ponies on Assateague and maybe some friendly dolphins in the ocean. Sunsets are particularly beautiful from out in the water.

The lobby of the Coconut Malorie Hotel offers a breathtaking statement of marble, spaciousness and elegance – along with the exotic touch of plants and Haitian art – that makes it one of the many beautiful hotels to visit in Ocean City.

ACCOMMODATIONS

An overview of Ocean City would not be complete without some mention of its myriad hotels, motels and restaurants. The ocean and the beach have always been a part of this world, but it wasn't until Isaac Coffin opened "The Rhode Island Inn" that the resort town took its first step in becoming what it is today. The history of Ocean City is inextricably interwoven with the history of its cottages, hotels and eating establishments.

Like Ocean City, the key to the local accommodations is diversity. The wide variety of hotels and restaurants on the island both reflect and are responsible for the unique faces of the three main areas of Ocean City: Old Town, Midtown and Upper Ocean City.

In Old Town, the hotels are large and rambling, cottages are small and quaint, with pitched rooflines and neat yards. The clapboard hotels sit close to or right on the boardwalk. With large verandas and porches, places like the Plim Plaza, the Lankford and Harrison Hall emphasize the relaxed and comfortable feeling of an Eastern Shore village.

Old Town is also the home of two of Ocean City's prestigious Bed and Breakfasts. Annabell's, a Cape Cod clapboard house, sits right on the beach; it's softly painted exterior and brightly lit interiors replete with wicker convey a home-like atmosphere. His Honor's Place is the boyhood home of long time Mayor Harry Kelley. It was turned into a bed and breakfast in 1987 as a way to preserve the home of one of the town's most popular mayors.

When it comes to food, you can't miss the classic boardwalk fare like pizza, ice cream, saltwater taffy, burgers, franks or maybe a flying-fruit fantasy. Anything you can carry while you walk is standard etiquette. Or maybe you'll want to journey over to bayside to the casual ambience of M.R. Ducks for drinks and conversation with the regulars.

For a more serious dining experience in Old Town, take in Phillips Beach Plaza. A restored hotel and restaurant, Phillips offers a variety of first rate seafood dishes with superb service, all in a plush Victorian setting.

In Midtown, the apartments, motels and hotels are more widely spaced, some strung along the beach and others perched on Coastal Highway or bayside. More family oriented, the sleeping establishments in this part of town are more modern in design. Walking along the beach, one can see the rows of geometrically-shaped balconies, all with a gorgeous view of the beach and the ocean. The Dunes Manor Hotel, sitting squarely on the beach, exemplifies the best of the old and the new here with her elegant Victorian-theme interiors, coupled with a traditional wide veranda with high-backed rockers for lazy evenings by the sea. Midtown is quieter, more slowly paced the farther north one gets from the heart of Old Town.

For a great evening of dining with the family, experience Phillips Crab House in Midtown. Phillips Restaurants, with their eclectic decor, have been a staple of Ocean City diets for years. Here you can enjoy succulent seafood or you can get a table piled high with piping hot steamed crabs.

Uptown Ocean City is the newer part of town and offers a totally different feel in its hotels and restaurants. Hotels like the Sheraton and the Carousel loom high above the beach and offer breathtaking views of points north and south as well as sights of the bay on the west. The rooms are elegant and stately, while outdoor beach grills and patios swarm with sunbathers and children carrying pails and inflated rafts to the edge of the sea.

Reflections, in the Holiday Inn, offers an elegant French ambience with a variety of gourmet French and American selections on the menu. The Hobbit, on bayside, is casual yet elegant, with marvelous homemade desserts and a beautiful view of the bay. Or you could sit back and enjoy a superb sunset at B.J.'s on the Water, while you sip cold drinks and meet interesting people. And, Fager's Island, on bayside, offers a casual outdoor raw bar and deck dining as well as an indoor restaurant/cafe that serves light fare. A more formal dining experience is available too, with a menu that is unmatched locally and a wine list that is one of the finest in the state of Maryland.

Ocean City's restaurants and cafes, menus and drinks offer something for any mood or whim. Check around, experiment; it's all part of the fun of having so much from which to choose.

There is so much more, you could spend a lifetime trying to see it all. Nevertheless, Ocean City never makes it difficult to decide with the variety of accommodations it offers. No matter what your taste, you're bound to find a place that's exactly right for you.

Phillips Seafood House, in Upper Ocean City, serves a variety of delectable seafood dishes in a comfortable surrounding with many different types of decor.

A restaurant with a long tradition in Ocean City is Phillips Crab House. Anchored in Midtown, Phillips prides itself on hearty seafood meals for the entire family. One of the largest restaurants in the country, the Crab House can seat 1500 hungry seafood lovers.

Phillips Beach Plaza Hotel is a restored hotel that sits on the boardwalk at 13th Street. The plush Victorian setting of the hotel and its restaurant (below) is elegant, and the seafood specialties on the menu are the pick of both the bay and the ocean.

Hooper's Crab and Seafood House offers a unique dining experience and is a must to see when visiting Ocean City. This huge barn-like building sits right on the bay, overlooking a panoramic view of the Ocean City skyline. The ambience of the interior is fascinating; every area is covered with antiques and unusual artifacts. Dining on the deck on a warm summer night sets the mood for a most enjoyable vacation.

One of the few Bed & Breakfasts in Ocean City, Annabell's charms visitors with its wicker furnishings and bright, sun-lit interiors. Sitting right on the beach, this Cape Cod structure retains the cozy warmth of its New England counterparts.

An evening party takes place in the shadows of the Sheraton. An architecturally stunning structure that rises high from the beach in Upper Ocean City, the Sheraton Ocean City Resort and Conference Center offers a wide array of luxurious features. Boasting several conference rooms and ballrooms, a health spa, gift shop and game room as well as a wide variety of eating and drinking establishments, the Sheraton is a perfect place to hold a conference or maybe just spend a few days at the ocean. The rooms are luxurious and full of space and offer some of the most spectacular views of the beach.

The Holiday Inn Oceanfront, at 67th Street, provides elegant yet relaxed rooms, all with a balcony overlooking the ocean. Enjoy the jacuzzis, hot tubs or pools, or walk out on the beach and enjoy the sun and sand. Reflections (below) is one of Ocean City's most elegant restaurants with an extensive menu that specializes in French and American cuisine.

Harrison Hall (above) and Plim Plaza (below) each offer comfortable surroundings right on the beach in Old Town. Enjoy spacious front porches where you can rock your time away watching the flow of the boardwalk. Convenient to all the attractions in Old Town, these hotels retain the small-town hospitality that has been so long connected with Ocean City's finest.

The Carousel Hotel, at 118th Street, boasts amenities that provide for year-round enjoyment. With lighted tennis courts, a heated, indoor pool and complete health spa, the beach becomes just one of a number of attractions at the resort hotel. Seasons Restaurant (below), provides great service and an attractive menu at the Carousel.

One of the most unique features in Ocean City is the Carousel's indoor ice rink. The town's only rink, it is open all year and complements the hotel's other attractions for those who are inclined to sports and recreation.

Harrison's Harbor Watch (above) overlooks the many sailing crafts that cross the inlet on their way to the bay. At Fager's Island Restaurant (below) you can enjoy the vibrant colors of the sunset and the gardens at the casual bistro or the outside deck. A formal dining room with a view of the bay is also available.

One of North Ocean City's famous night spots is located in the Ramada Inn, (formerly The Fenwick Inn) at 138th Street. O.C.'s only rooftop restaurant and lounge offers magnificent views of both ocean and bay. The award-winning Lookout Restaurant (above) is one of the nation's first to offer a complete low-cholesterol menu in addition to a full selection of seafood, steaks and light French fare. The Lookout Lounge (below) seats 450 and is known for providing some of the finest showband entertainment on the East Coast.

A morning mist settles on the large fishing boats in West Ocean City. Just on the other side of the Route 50 bridge, West Ocean City harbors the commercial fishing fleet.

SURROUNDING AREAS

For those who need to recover from a little too much sun, or maybe just want a day or two from the beach, Ocean City's surrounding neighborhoods offer a staggering array of choices, from delightfully planned new developments to small towns loaded with historic sites and significance.

Just on the other side of the Route 50 bridge, West Ocean City harbors the heart of the town's commercial fishing fleet. Filled with old-style charm and rugged atmosphere, the docks and piers are swarming with characters straight out of your favorite fishing stories. When you get close and look into the eyes of these sailor/fishermen, you're bound to see the mysterious twinkle that reflects their love for the salty air and misty waters that permeate every nook of this part of town.

Further north, after crossing the Route 90 span, you'll find the signs leading to Ocean Pines, a newer development of year round residences tucked under the cool shadows of the lush pine woods. The planners of this community have successfully maintained the feel of the quiet Eastern Shore atmosphere while capturing the finest in waterfront living along a series of canals and riverfronts. Boasting everything from tennis courts and pools to a championship golf course, Ocean Pines is a place for those who want to experience the special bay flavor of the Eastern Shore while living with all the modern conveniences.

The rest of Worcester County lies ahead for those looking for "undiscovered areas" hidden away from the beach. Across the inlet from Ocean City is Assateague Island, famous for its ponies who have roamed the dunes and grasslands here for centuries. Assateague is a state and federal complex laid out with hiking, camping and canoeing facilities that allows the naturalist to wander the wonderfully undisturbed land of this fragile barrier island. The National Park Service offers a series of programs on the natural and historical aspects of bay and beach life.

Eight miles out of Ocean City is the historic little town of Berlin. Named after the slurred pronunciation of "Burley Inn," the town is a gigantic museum of historically preserved buildings and homes. The Calvin B. Taylor home, on Main Street, is a museum devoted to the history of the town.

Though historically cherished, Berlin is a living town too. Many of the private homes in town are architectural delights and many house antique shops. The Atlantic Hotel, in the center of town, has been restored to its Victorian splendor and offers excellent accommodations and a wonderful menu.

Snow Hill, the Worcester County seat, lies a little over twenty miles away. A town rich in tradition and slower in pace, its Colonial, Federal and Victorian era homes still look down on quiet streets. Local artisans are constantly showing off their wares, many made in the traditions of centuries past. The Julia A. Purnell Museum charts the county's history and the Nassawango Iron Furnace Historic Site pays tribute to the once thriving local industry.

Still further, day tripping will take you to other historic towns like Easton and St. Michaels. There are two state parks on Route 113 toward Pocomoke (on the Pocomoke River), with a natural environment that is home to beautiful cypress trees and refuge for majestic birdlife including eagles, egrets and hawks.

It's startling, in the hustle and bustle of Ocean City, that the small town atmosphere of the surrounding area has not just survived, but flourished. That it has done so is a tribute to the inhabitants of these small towns and villages and a blessing for the visitor to Ocean City that they can still appreciate the streets and buildings, as well as the atmosphere and traditions, of the southern part of the Eastern Shore.

The sun rises on the expansive, unspoiled beach of Assateague Island. The state and federal complex is laid out with hiking, canoeing and camping facilities that allow visitors to explore the unique natural landscape of a barrier island. The famous Assateague ponies munch on marsh grass at sunrise (below).

Berlin (above) is a living museum of historic and restored homes. Many of the homes operate as antique shops. Snow Hill (below), the Worcester County seat, was founded in 1642 and is the home of a variety of small-town charms from arts and crafts to boating and architectural highlights.

The sun brushes pink and blue pastels across the sky and sea at sunrise. Ocean City is the home of Maryland's most dramatic sunrises and sunsets; no two are alike and there are thousands of spots from which one can enjoy them.